FERRARI RACING –
A PICTORIAL HISTORY

Ferrari's 1967 330 P4 spider is unquestionably one of the most beautiful sports racing cars of all time.

FERRARI RACING

A PICTORIAL HISTORY

Colin Goodwin

with photographs from the
National Motor Museum, Beaulieu

The Crowood Press

First published in 1997 by
The Crowood Press Ltd
Ramsbury, Marlborough
Wiltshire SN8 2HR

British Library Cataloguing-in-Publication Data
A catalogue record for this book is available from the British
Library

ISBN 1 86126 091 1

Typeface used: Times.

Typeset and designed by
D & N Publishing
Membury Business Park, Lambourn Woodlands
Hungerford, Berkshire.

Printed and bound by The Bath Press.

Contents

A History of Ferrari

ENZO FERRARI: FROM RACER TO THE SCUDERIA FERRARI

On a summer's day in 1908 a father took his two sons to watch a motor race just outside Bologna in northern Italy. The race was the Coppa Florio, run over ten laps of a 32.8-mile (52.7km) road course. The winner of this gruelling event was Felice Nazarro driving a bellowing Fiat. Those early motor races were beyond the imagination of today's motor-racing fans: the roads were unsurfaced so spectators and drivers were showered with stones and covered in dust, the cars were often powered by huge unsilenced engines, and the racing was dangerous.

However, the race made a lasting impression on the youngest of the two boys. Ten-year-old Enzo Ferrari had wanted to be an opera singer, but the noise and the sight of those heroes throwing their roaring machines around the corners changed his mind and he determined there and then that he was going to be a racing driver. The world of opera probably doesn't mourn his decision, but the motor-racing world would certainly have noticed his absence.

Enzo's father ran an engineering business manufacturing gangways and locomotive sheds for the railways. He had hoped that both his sons would have gone to university and become engineers but World War I put an end to those hopes, Father Alfredo and Enzo's brother Alfredo Jnr both dying of battlefield-induced illnesses and leaving Enzo at the end of hostilities lonely and depressed. Things began to come right for Enzo when he found a job in Turin delivering vehicles for an entrepreneur who converted ex-military vehicles into cars. Through this job he met Ugo Sivocci, a young man who did similar work for car-maker CMN. But in addition to delivering cars, Sivocci tested them and competed in motor races, manufacturers having already caught on to the fact that racing sold the cars they made. The young Enzo Ferrari was taken on as Sivocci's assistant, and before long he, too, was given the chance to drive his employer's products in competition. In a hillclimb between Palma and the mountain village of Berceto, Enzo came fourth in his class. The winner was Antonio Ascari, a name that Ferrari would meet again later in his life.

From there, Ferrari and Sivocci took a new CMN racer down to Sicily for the famous Targa Florio road race; Ferrari's race was full of incident and he came in ninth. The next year he and Sivocci were both at Alfa Romeo and Ferrari's future was apparently all but settled, though not as a racing driver: although he won many domestic events, in the top level grand prix he was outclassed. In 1929 he formed his own racing team to run Alfa Romeos, and returned to his home town of Modena; thus Scuderia Ferrari was born. Over the next five years Ferrari hired the great talents of the time such as Achille Varzi and Tazio Nuvolari, and ran the team which after the 1932 season became the official Alfa Romeo works team. The cars wore a distinctive badge, a prancing horse set against a yellow background; a similar badge was once to be found on the fuselage of Italian fighter ace Francesco Baracca's plane – but whatever its origins, it is now one of the most treasured motoring insignia around the world.

In 1938 Alfa brought its racing efforts back home and offered Ferrari the job of team manager. He took it, but not for long, years of being his own boss making it difficult for him to be under one. At the end of the year he left Alfa Romeo for the last time and went back to Modena where he set up a design and engineering company. Although part of his leaving deal with Alfa prohibited him from competing for four years, the new company produced a couple of 1.5-litre eight-cylinder racers from a stack of Fiat parts. Since these cars would compete in a different class to any other Alfa, the project was overlooked by the Milanese maker. Besides, when the cars ran – in the last Mille Miglia before the war in April 1940 – they wore neither the Ferrari name nor the prancing horse.

During the war, Ferrari produced high quality ball-bearing grinding machines as well as aero engine parts. At a later point in the war the factory was moved from the hot target of Modena to the village of Maranello, twelve miles away; it is now known as the home of Ferrari and probably always will be.

When the war ended, Enzo Ferrari turned his thoughts back to cars. He had a factory full of machine tools, the pick of talent from an area with an international reputation for engineering excellence, and over twenty years of experience in racing and preparing high performance cars. The most emotive name in racing history was about to exert its influence.

THE RACING: THE BEGINNING

On 11 May 1947 the first Ferrari lined up for its first race. Franco Cortese and his Ferrari 125 S didn't finish the race at Piacenza – the fuel pump broke – but the world saw what was to come and the new car was truly amazing for a vehicle produced from scratch in a war-torn country. The 125 S was fitted with a single overhead cam V12 displacing 1.5 litres: multiply 125 (the cc of each cylinder) by twelve and you arrive at the engine's total cubic capacity. This formula worked until the late 1960s.

Victory for the Scuderia Ferrari was not far off, however, because two weeks after the Piacenza race Cortese took the 125 S to victory in a race in Rome. The horse had started running, and in July the great Tazio Nuvolari joined the Scuderia.

Over the winter of 1947 the 125 S grew in displacement to 1.9 litres, and this led to a type name-change, to 159 S. Over the years Ferrari built a huge variety of different racers, often in very small numbers; for example, as soon as the 159 S was built it was followed by the 166 S. The new Tipo 166 had a fantastic year in 1948, winning both the Mille Miglia and the Targa Floria road races, an achievement which really couldn't be bettered – except, of course, for winning the Le Mans twenty-four hours race. Then in 1949 the Ferrari 166 MM (for Mille Miglia) won the Targa, driven by Clemente Biondetti – who had won the 1948 race – and Aldo Benedetti. Biondetti also won the Mille Miglia, this time with Ettore Salani as co-driver. But an even greater victory was that Luigi Chinetti and Lord Selsdon won the great French race, also in a 166 MM. Chinetti played a lead role in the Ferrari story, largely because it was he who brought Ferrari into the United States and onto its race tracks – and later, into the garages of America's rich and famous.

THE 1950s

In 1950 the first World Driver's Championship was staged for Formula One cars; this was really the start of grand prix racing as we know it today. As well as the 125 S sports cars, Ferrari had built the Type 125 single-seater racing car, though the car didn't make its appearance until late 1948. Like the 125 S, the 125 grand prix car had a 1.5-litre V12, though this time it was supercharged to give 225bhp. Then in 1949 Alfa decided to bow out, its ageing Tipo 158 F1 car now stretched to its mechanical limits and far too thirsty. This meant that the 1949 season became virtually a walkover for Ferrari and Maserati, with Ferrari winning nineteen of the year's most important races, as well as victories in the Formula Two class with an unsupercharged version of the Giaocchini Colombo-designed V12 engine.

For the 1950 season the 125 F1 gained twin camshafts per bank, and twin-stage supercharging that brought power up to 315bhp. Alfa Romeo once again fielded its ageing Tipo 158s, uprated for the last race of the year – the Italian Grand Prix at Monza – into the Tipo 159. Ferrari also introduced a new car at that meeting: realizing that Alfa Romeo was at a severe disadvantage with its thirsty supercharged engine, Ferrari had decided to build a naturally aspirated V12 of 4.5 litres. Colombo had by this time defected to Alfa Romeo, so his assistant at Ferrari, Aurelio Lampredi, was put in charge of creating the new long-block V12 engine. Before the 4.5-litre 375 F1 made its debut at Monza, a 3.3-litre version had raced at the Belgium Grand Prix at Spa, proving to be reliable but dismally slow. A 4.1-litre version followed this, and cars of this calibre were raced at the Grand Prix des Nations at Geneva by Antonio Ascari (son of Antonio) and Luigi Villoresi. Villoresi crashed, killing several spectators, and Ascari's engine blew. Ascari's 375 F1 also blew an engine at Monza, but he took over team mate Dorino Serafini's car and finished second.

Things looked promising for the Scuderia in 1951, fuel consumption apparently being Alfa's big problem again. Alfa did have the great Juan Manuel Fangio in its team, however, and won the first three grand prix of the season, Fangio taking two, Guiseppe Farina one. But at the fourth race, the British Grand Prix at Silverstone, Ferrari chalked up the first of many F1 victories. The driver was

Froilan Gonzalez, a mountain of a man from Argentina nicknamed the Pampas Bull.

In 1952 the championship was run to F2 regulations as there were not enough competitive Formula One cars around to compete for the title. Ferrari used its F2 car, but instead of the usual V12 engine, this 500 F2 model used a new Lampredi-designed 2.0-litre four-cylinder engine. The combination of this car and Alberto Ascari proved to be unbeatable. Piero Taruffi in another Ferrari 500 won the first grand prix, the Swiss, but Ascari subsequently won the remaining six races and scooped the World Championship for Ferrari – and the following year was almost equally successful for the Maranello team. He started by winning, and repeated this victory in the next two races, making it nine wins in succession. He also scored another two wins in 1953 to bring him and Ferrari their second World Championship.

In 1954 the rules changed again, with 2.5 litres being the upper capacity limit for the unblown F1 cars. Ferrari had its new 625 F1 car ready, but it was going to have to face the challenge of Mercedes who were returning to the fray – and worse still for Ferrari was that the Germans had Fangio driving its cars. Ferrari did not have a good year. The 625 was uncompetitive, and Fangio swept to World Championship victory in the silver Mercedes-Benz. The story was the same in 1955, with Fangio again winning the championship for Mercedes. His team-mate Stirling Moss was second in an identical W196.

The next year Mercedes did not compete. The company had pulled out of racing after one of its cars crashed into the crowd at Le Mans, killing over seventy spectators. Ascari had been killed in 1955 testing a Ferrari sports car at Monza, so Fangio took his place. In 1956 and 1957 Ferrari ran Lancia/Ferrari hybrids. Lancia was in financial trouble and Ferrari wasn't having any success with his 625, so he took on the Lancia D50s – although it was Fangio's skill, rather than the cars' ability, that took the 1956 championship for the team. Fangio left the team after the season's close, citing Enzo's aloofness from the drivers as one of the main reasons for his decision. The 1957 season was a fruitless one for the team; and Fangio won his last World Championship, this time in a Maserati 250F. New to the team was Mike Hawthorn, the 'gentleman' racing driver personified: he always raced wearing a bow tie, he was good looking, and he made sure that he thoroughly enjoyed his racing.

In 1958 Ferrari had a new racer for the season, the 246 Dino, named after Ferrari's beloved son Dino who had died in 1956. The 246 Dino took Hawthorn to the World Championship, although he had in fact only won one race to Moss's four. Tragically the charismatic Englishman did not have long to enjoy his triumph: Hawthorn crashed his Jaguar on the Guildford bypass in January 1959 and was killed instantly. This was the second tragedy for Ferrari in twelve months, as fellow Englishman, Ferrari driver and a close friend of Hawthorn's, Peter Collins, was killed at the German Grand Prix earlier in 1958.

Another Englishman, Tony Brooks, joined the Scuderia for 1959, the year that marked a great change in Formula One. Jack Brabham won the championship that year in a rear-engined Cooper. Enzo Ferrari had for several years been scornful of the Cooper saying 'The horse pulls the cart, not the other way around'; but in the coming decade he would have to laugh at that comment.

Throughout the fifties Ferrari sports cars raced all over the world, in the hands of wealthy amateurs, gentleman racers, and also entered in private teams such as the North American Racing Team of Luigi Chinetti (Ferrari's old friend and Le Mans winner), and Jacques Swater's Ecurie Francorchamps. Jaguar made Le Mans its territory in the 1950s with its famous C- and D-types, although Ferrari sneaked wins in 1954 with Gonzalez and Maurice Trintignant in a 375 Plus, and with Oliver Gendebien and American Phil Hill in a 250TR – known as the Testarossa due to its red valve covers. On the other hand, Ferrari practically owned the Mille Miglia in the fifties, losing out only to a Lancia in 1954 and to Mercedes in 1955, when Moss and Jenkinson had their famous victory. That great race was last run in anger in 1957, when the Marquis de Portago crashed his Ferrari, killing a group of eleven spectators.

THE 1960s

The sixties started with Ferrari failing to score a single international victory. Cooper had proved that the front-engined F1 car was on its way out, and Ferrari's 1960 season 246 Dinos did little to disprove this. Ferrari changed its numbering system for these V6 racing cars, so that the first two digits referred to the cubic capacity, and the last to the number of cylinders: therefore 2.4-litre, six-cylinder. The same system ended up on the road cars from the 1970s onwards.

The 1960 sports car season was more successful. Gendebien and Belgian journalist Paul Frere took a 250 TR to victory at Le Mans in June, starting a five-year run of success for the Italian team at the Sarthe circuit. In fact the 1960s would prove to be one of the golden eras of sports car racing, with Ferrari producing some of its most wonderful and exciting cars and beginning its epic struggles with Ford's new GT40 racer. Things could have been very different, however, because in 1963 Enzo Ferrari was in secret negotiation with the Ford Motor Company to sell 90 per cent of his road car business and 10 per cent of his racing team to the American giant. In the end the deal wasn't right for the autocratic Italian, but it did point to the future, when Fiat would take a big share in the company in 1969. Meanwhile if Ford couldn't buy it, it determined to beat Ferrari on the track, and this was the reasoning behind the birth of the GT40 racer.

Back in F1, by the end of the 1960 season Ferrari had decided to 'push the cart with the horse', and for the 1961 grand prix season had made ready the 156 F1: this beautiful little shark-nosed open wheeler was the company's first mid-engined GP car, and with it, Phil Hill won the championship and became the first American to win the title. Sadly the season came to a close on a tragic note when the popular Wolfgang 'Taffy' von Trips, also in a 156, collided with Jim Clark at the Italian Grand Prix: Clark was unhurt, but von Trips was thrown out and the car careered into the crowd; von Trips was killed, as were eleven spectators.

Over the winter Ferrari's chief engineer Carlo Chiti and his team manager Tavoni walked out and, as might be expected, the following year failed to match the previous one. In 1962, too, Ferrari failed to win a grand prix, and at the end of the season Hill left, unhappy with the dreadful handling of that year's car. For 1963 Ferrari signed John Surtees, the multiple world motorcycle champion. Ferrari had run Norton and Rudge motorcycle racing teams before the war, and considered that motorcycle racers made naturally good racing drivers – and Surtees certainly didn't let the old man down. He won Ferrari's only grand prix in 1963 at the Nurburgring.

For 1964 Ferrari had the 158 F1, a 1.5-litre V8-engined semi-monocoque car. The season started well with a win for Surtees at the Syracuse Grand Prix but then Ferrari fortunes took a downturn – until the Nurburgring which Surtees won for the second year running. A month later he won in Italy, and then went on to clinch the championship in Mexico, with a bit of bad luck for Graham Hill and Jim Clark. The Mexican race was interesting because the Ferraris didn't run in their customary red. Enzo was in dispute with the FIA at the time, over the homologation of the new 250 LM sports car, and as a gesture of indignation he had the cars entered and run in Mexico under Chinetti's NART flag.

The 1965 season was the last for the puny 1.5-litre cars: they hardly matched the previous season, with Surtees and team-mate Lorenzo Bandini managing only fifth and six places in the championship that year. For 1966 Ferrari was back with a V12 after a long absence, a fabulous 3.0-litre V12 F1 car named the 312 F1. Sadly the car wasn't that good, and only two grand prix wins between 1966 and 1969 was a big disappointment, particularly as that was with talented drivers such as Chris Amon and Jacky Ickx. Surtees had left the team in 1966 after a serious disagreement and had gone to Honda; Bandini perished in a dreadful fire at the 1967 Monaco Grand Prix.

Away from the grand prix circus, Ferrari sports cars were busy establishing a legend, carving a place in the history books, and as they did so they promoted the Ferrari road cars, often very closely related to the racing models. None was more so than the 250 GT: this model became known as the 250 SWB (for short wheel base) – although it was was never officially tagged as such – and was one of the last cars that you could buy, stick numbers on, drive to the races and then win in – and we're not talking here of little club races either. For example, Stirling Moss drove Rob Walker's 250 SWB to victory in the 1961 Goodwood TT. Walker was typical of the private entrant, many of whom clinched often convoluted deals with the factory for racing models.

After the SWB came the 250 GTO, now one of the most valuable cars in the world. The GTO raced and won over all the international circuits, and to hear its 3.0-litre V12 was a privilege; it was truly the front-engined sports car taken to its most beautiful and purposeful.

But eventually even the 250 GT had to make way for the mid-engined revolution: it was replaced by the 250 LM, the car that was getting Ferrari into trouble with the FIA. They contended that the name was misleading, for in fact only the prototype of this twelve-cylinder GT was actually a 3.0-litre, all the production versions being 3.3-litre, which meant that they should really have been called 275 LMs. Besides this, the cars had odd-numbered chassis, indicating that they were actually road cars (the racers' chassis having even numbers), and indeed, many LMs were used on the road. By the time the FIA finally decided that the car should be in the GT class in 1966, it was no longer competitive; before that it had to run as a sports prototype, where it didn't stand much chance against rivals such as Ferrari's 275 P and 330 P prototypes. That said, Masten Gregory and Jochen Rindt won the 1965 Le Mans in a 250 LM, the last time that Ferrari has won the French classic.

The final half of the 1960s brought the epic Ford versus Ferrari battles at Le Mans. Ford was pumping huge resources into its GT40 programme, a policy which in its early years didn't seem to be paying off. Then in 1966 it all came right for the Americans when Fords came in first, second and third with Amon and McLaren driving the winning car. Ford won in 1967, 1968 and 1969, in spite of Ferrari putting up a strong challenge with one of the most gorgeous racing cars in history: the 1967 330 P4. Its 4.0-litre V12 produced a strong 450bhp at 8,200rpm, and although Le Mans might have eluded the Italians, at Daytona in 1967 the Ferrari prototypes made a huge impression. Not only did Ferrari fill the first three places, but they crossed the line in close formation thereby amply paying Ford back for the first, second and third across-the-line finish at Le Mans the previous year. P4s also came first and second at Monza – but there the winning spree ended.

Le Mans in 1967 was a classic. The factory entered four P4s, with the usual independent teams also competing in earlier P3s (albeit uprated to P4 spec). However, this big effort was still not enough to stop AJ Foyt and Dan Gurney's Ford from finishing first, ahead of Ludovico Scarfiotti and Michael Parkes in the factory P4, and Willy Mairesse and 'Beurlys' third in their P4 (Jean Blaton used the pseudonym 'Beurlys' to prevent his industrialist father finding out what he did for a hobby).

THE 1970s AND 1980s

The 1970s saw Ferrari's F1 at last claim victory in F1 competition, though the decade was well on its way before success finally arrived. Lotus were the cars to beat in the late 1960s and early 1970s: Colin Chapman's creative genius was in full flood, with Jochen Rindt posthumously winning the 1970 championship (he died at Monza and no one could beat his points score) in the advanced Lotus 72. Ferrari used its 312 B that year, with 'B' standing for 'Boxer', the term used for a flat or horizontally opposed engine. Ferrari had briefly tried the layout before: Bandini had driven a 1.5-litre twelve-cylinder Boxer-engined car in practice at Monza in 1964, and also later during 1965, though it had never proved a winner. Jacky Ickx notched up the 312 B's first win in Austria, followed by wins in Canada and Mexico, with team-mate Clay Regazzoni winning the Italian Grand Prix, a considerable achievement as this was his first year in F1.

The 1971 and 1972 seasons saw a few wins for Ickx and Mario Andretti, but there were none at all the following year. Meanwhile in sports cars Ferrari came up supreme in the 1972 Championship of Makes, demolishing Alfa Romeo opposition with its 312 P sports racer; these cars were driven by an equally strong team of drivers, aces such as Ronnie Petersen, Mario Andretti, Jacky Ickx and Brian Redman. In 1972 Ferrari also won its last Targa Florio, with Arturo Merzario and Sandro Munari driving. The 1970s heralded the beginning of Porsche domination in sports car racing: although Ferrari's powerful 512 M and S sports prototypes put up a big fight at Le Mans, they couldn't match the Porsches.

In 1974 the Austrian Niki Lauda joined the F1 team; he took a couple of victories in the 312 B3. In 1975 along came the new 312 T ('T' for 'transversale', referring to the transverse gearbox) and, for the first time since Surtees in 1964, a Ferrari-mounted driver won the World Championship. The following season started well, but then Lauda had a very bad crash at the Nurburgring, in which he nearly died – although he was back in the car remarkably soon after this. He was back in top form for the 1977 season, scooping the Driver's Championship for the second time.

Ferrari's final glory in the 1970s was Jody Sheckter's championship in 1979, when he was team-mate to Gilles Villeneuve. Gilles Villeneuve was like a son to Enzo: he was young, he was a fighter and in a racing car he had incredible speed, and as far as Ferrari was concerned, who could go fast was all-important. Villeneuve's car control was in a different league to his rivals'. It needed to be. Few will forget the sight of the young Canadian flinging his turbocharged 126 C from lock to lock, often half on the grass; but even his genius could not win a World Championship in the evil car. Things looked more promising for 1982: the new 126 C2 was a big improvement and Villeneuve and the young Didier Pironi were among the very best drivers. But then on 9 May in Belgium came tragedy, when in the last few minutes of qualifying, Villeneuve's Ferrari clipped the rear of a slower car and launched into the air. Villeneuve was killed instantly. Enzo Ferrari never showed his emotion and was widely thought of as a cold man, but in private he cried over Villeneuve's death. Nor did Ferrari's fortunes improve, because later in the year Pironi's career was ended by a serious accident in Germany. All in all it was a terrible year for Ferrari.

THE FUTURE

Ferrari has not won a World Championship since 1979, and this is not only bad news for Ferrari and for Italy, but bad news for Formula One: Grand Prix racing without a blood-red Ferrari challenging for the lead is unthinkable. But the tide is turning, and the politics, which in the past have so often played too big a part at Maranello, now seem to be under control. The all-powerful Italian press is not being allowed to make all the decisions, and the right people are behind the team. And in Michael Schumacher Ferrari has the best racing driver in the world.

The Thirties and Forties

Enzo Ferrari just inside the gates at the Maranello factory. It looks just the same today. Ferrari died in 1988, but anyone visiting the factory will feel his spirit in the atmosphere: for a racing enthusiast it is a holy place, and always will be.

Tazio Nuvolari in one of the Scuderia Ferrari's 2.3-litre 8C (eight-cylinder) Alfas at the 1931 Targa Florio. He is entering Cerda and passing the pits that were used until the last running of the race in 1973.

Luigi Villoresi in a supercharged 1.5-litre Ferrari leads Baron De Gaffenreid's Maserati 4CLT in the 1949 British Grand Prix at the then new Silverstone airfield circuit.

The great Tazio Nuvolari in his 8C 2.3 MM at the 1933 Mille Miglia; beside him is his riding mechanic and navigator Compagnoni. The pair won the race.

The Borzacchini/Bucchi Alfa 8C 2.3 MM being serviced in Bologna during the 1933 Mille Miglia. Just to finish the gruelling 1,000-mile race was an achievement. This pair failed to complete the course.

Achille Varzi and his mechanic Tabachi in their much modified Alfa P2 Grand Prix car; this photograph shows just how challenging were conditions on events such as the Targa Florio. The year is 1930; ten years earlier Enzo Ferrari had finished second in the Targa.

This race at Montlhéry in 1934 was an historic occasion as it was the first time that the awesome Auto Union and Mercedes Silver Arrows raced. It wasn't an auspicious start, however, as the race turned out to be an outstanding success for Scuderia Ferrari with an Alfa Romeo one-two-three. Louis Chiron (number twelve) was the winner.

Luigi Fagioli in the pits in the 1933 Gran Premio d'Italia at Monza. The 'Abruzzi Robber', as Fagioli was nicknamed, finished first in the race in his P3 2.6 Alfa.

The Honourable Brian Lewis in the Scuderia Ferrari P3 2.6. Judging from the policeman in the background, the venue is obviously in the British Isles, and experts in policemen's helmets will guess correctly at the Isle of Man. This is the 1934 Mannin Moar, in which Lewis scored a win.

An Alfa Romeo 2.9-litre with an un-named driver rounds a house in the 1934 Mannin Moar on the Isle of Man. Note the twin wheels at the rear, a trick more often seen at hill climbs for the extra grip.

Louis Chiron led the 1934 Monaco Grand Prix from the start, then almost at the finish line he over-cornered and thus let Guy Moll through to the flag. History repeated itself in 1970 when Jack Brabham slid off at almost the last corner, allowing Jochen Rindt to win.

The stunning Alfa 8C 3.8-litre is pushed out of a Nurburgring pit garage for the 1936 German Grand Prix; its driver was Count Tonino Brivio. The car is actually from 1935, as the Scuderia's 1936 cars all had twelve-cylinder engines.

Count Trossi was fastest in practice for the 1934 Monaco Grand Prix in his 2.9-litre Alfa Romeo Type B, but retired on the ninety-fifth lap with transmission failure. Wrestling these big single-seaters around the principality's streets must have been exhausting.

(Left) This monster is the 1935 Alfa Romeo Bimotore, one of racing's oddballs. As you would expect, it has two engines, both 2.9-litre straight-eight engines producing 540bhp and nearly 200mph (322km). Team manager Enzo Ferrari is behind the car to the left of the fedora-wearer.

(Below) A famous and frequently reproduced photograph of Louis Chiron on his way to second place in the 1935 Grand Prix of Dieppe. The car is a 3.2-litre Alfa Romeo.

Le Mans 1949 with Luigi Chinetti and Lord Selsdon in a 166 MM: they won. Note the trees, the lack of protection and the proximity of the spectators: this was racing in its purest form.

Raymond Mays had started the 1949 British Grand Prix in the first of the Thin Wall Ferraris, but then handed the 125 F1 over to Ken Richardson (here). Unfortunately on this occasion Richardson lost control of this unforgiving model and crashed into a group of spectators at Silverstone's Abbey Curve. Thankfully, no one was seriously injured.

(Below) Even exotic Ferraris found their way onto the club scene back then. Imagine turning up at a meeting at Castle Combe today with a two-year-old Ferrari F1 car. Surely W. Dobson in his 125 F1 isn't about to race the smoker in the F4 Cooper behind?

The year is 1949 and the occasion the Dutch Grand Prix at the coastal circuit of Zandvoort; Luigi Villoresi won the event in a Ferrari 125. This is team-mate Ascari.

The Fifties

Luigi Villoresi in the supercharged 1.5-litre 125 F1 in 1950. For the next season Ferrari went to a 4.5-litre naturally aspirated V12 which proved much more successful.

Ferrari notched up a large number of race wins with its 2.0-litre 500 Formula Two cars. Here a long line of them awaits the start of the 1950 Reims Formula Two race.

A somewhat puffy-cheeked Alberto Ascari pushes his 375 F1 round one of the corners on the Penya Rhin circuit just outside Barcelona in 1950. See how the spectators are well 'protected' by just one piece of rope: a disaster waiting to happen.

(Below) Juan Manuel Fangio in an Alfa 158 at the 1950 International Trophy at Silverstone. Fangio won the second heat, and came second in the final to Farina's similar car. It was the last year that the Alfas were able to dominate the Ferraris.

Luigi Villoresi sits in his Tipo 166 F2 car just before the start of an F2 race at Reims, his car as yet without numbers. In the race it wore number twenty-six. His particular race didn't last long as the Ferrari broke a de Dion tube on the first lap.

The 'Pampas Bull', Froilan Gonzalez, en route to a win at the 1951 British Grand Prix at Silverstone. It was Ferrari's first F1 victory. The 4.5-litre signalled the death of the 1.5-litre supercharged racing car.

Alberto Ascari in his 4.5-litre 375 F1 in 1951, with a young rival in a slightly smaller single-seater. Alberto's father Antonio was killed racing when his son was seven, and Alberto himself was killed in 1955 while testing a Ferrari sports racer.

Test session in Italy in 1951 for one of the Tipo 375 F1 cars. They were intended to capitalize on the supercharged 1.5-litre Alfa Romeo 158 and 159s, and in particular their exceptionally high fuel consumption. Froilan Gonzalez gave Ferrari its first grand prix in one, in the same year as this picture.

Piero Taruffi's 375 F1 parked at the side of the Pedralbes circuit during the 1951 Spanish Grand Prix. As can be seen, his Ferrari is suffering from a shortage of wheels: spot the gouged track surface.

(Above) Eugenio Castellotti climbs into his Lancia/Ferrari D50 for the 1956 British Grand Prix at Silverstone. In the deerstalker hat is the legendary journalist John Bolster; he would have been busy on the microphone as Castelotti's car was later taken over by de Portago. Peter Collins then took over his car.

(Left) In 1952–53 there were not enough competitive F1 machines to make a field, so F2 cars were run instead. This is Luigi Villoresi in a four-cylinder, 2.0-litre 500 F2 at the 1953 British Grand Prix. He retired with a broken gearbox.

(Opposite) The Alfa Romeo 159 – the final incarnation of the two-stage supercharged 1.5-litre F1 car – finally met its match in 1951. Here at Monza, Ascari's 375 Ferrari leads Fangio's Alfa: Ascari won, while Fangio's car holed a piston trying to keep up.

Judging by his trousers, it looks as if this driver is expecting rain. The car is a twelve-cylinder 225 S, which if the formula is used, works out as a 2.7-litre. It is the early 1950s, and the venue is most likely Silverstone.

A 225 S visits the pits during the 1952 Goodwood Nine Hours race. Racing was stopped at Goodwood in 1966, because of concerns regarding safety; visit it now and you will find it easy to imagine this scene, so little has the place changed.

Inside the cockpit of an early fifties' 500 F2 Ferrari. Note the gear lever on the left with the characteristic Ferrari reverse-lockout lever; the rev-counter had a 7,000rpm red line for the 2.0-litre four-cylinder engine.

Although a V12, the Ferrari twelve-cylinder is quite narrow thanks to its 60-degree angle. This 1952 sports-car engine (possibly in a 166 MM) wears three Weber carburettors. Spot the dual magnetos at the rear of the engine, one for each bank of cylinders.

Mike Hawthorn about to start in the 1953 Goodwood Trophy race. The words 'Thin Wall Special' refer to entrant Tony Vandervell's bearing company: Vandervell bought the car direct from the factory.

*Mike Hawthorn at the limit in a 4.1-litre 340 MM at the 1953
International Trophy at Silverstone. Several versions of the 340 were
made, including the M (for Mexico) and the America. At 300bhp the MM
was the most powerful.*

This road was more accustomed to the sound of racing motorcycles than a Ferrari V12. It is Douglas on the Isle of Man; the driver is Hans Ruesch, and the event is the 1953 Empire Trophy. The winner was Reg Parnell in an Aston DB3 S.

The closed 250 MM carried beautiful bodywork by Pininfarina. This car is at Le Mans in 1953, but the model did not perform well in this year, partly because Ferrari was concentrating on the bigger-engined cars.

A 750 Monza sits outside the works. This model first raced in 1954 and was the most successful of the four-cylinder Ferrari race cars. Ferrari's son Dino designed its bodywork.

A monster 375 MM is chased through the Esses at Le Mans by an Aston Martin, an American Cunningham and lastly a C-type Jaguar. Duncan Hamilton and Tony Rolt won this 1953 race in a C-type Jaguar.

*Froilan Gonzalez and Maurice Trintignant's race-weary 375 Plus tended
by proud mechanics after its victory in the 1954 twenty-four hour Le
Mans marathon. This was one year in the 1950s that Jaguar didn't win.*

*Three years on, and Gonzalez repeats his 1951 British Grand Prix win,
this time in a four-cylinder 625 F1. The portly Argentinian is a far cry
from today's lean, whippet-like drivers.*

Two 4.9-litre 375 Pluses wait in the rain before the 1954 Le Mans twenty-four-hour race. The cars were real monsters, producing 330bhp from their V12s. In the wet they must have truly concentrated the mind.

Although Ferraris are synonymous with wailing V12 engines, the company made a great variety of types. This 121 LM uses a 4.4-litre straight-six. Both of the two 121 LMs were rebodied after the 1955 season: one went to the US, the other to Britain.

Compare the cockpit of Froilan Gonzalez's 1954 'Super Squalo' with that of a modern grand prix car. Note also the fuel filler to the driver's right: these cars were mobile fuel tanks, the driver surrounded by high octane petrol.

*A Ferrari sports racer takes shape in the Scaglietti workshops in Modena.
Scaglietti built nearly all the racing Ferraris and many of the road cars. Old man
Scaglietti is one of the few men alive today who knew Enzo from the beginning.*

Eugenio Castellotti in critical trouble on the Monza banking in a Lancia/Ferrari D50 in the 1955 Italian Grand Prix. He was travelling at 170mph (275km/h) at the time the tyre exploded. Fortunately he was unhurt.

Guiseppe Farina in the 2.5-litre Super Squalo 555 at Spa in 1955. Although fastest in practice, his car was no match for the Mercedes of Fangio and Moss and he finished a distant third.

Ferrari's main rival, the Alfa Romeo 158, in the hands of one of the greatest talents of all time, Juan Manuel Fangio. Note the lack of protection in those days, and also the amount of muscle it took to drive these old cars – as can be seen from the master's biceps.

The ex-Pete Whitehead Ferrari 125 F1 at the Donington Collection. Whitehead was a wealthy farmer who could afford to indulge his passion for motor racing. Not that he was a playboy racer: he was quick, and had many good results on the continent.

Ferrari built cars with four, six and eight cylinders, but it is for the twelve-cylinder V engines that the company is most famed. This one sits in a 250 MM. The number 250 refers to the cubic capacity of one cylinder; multiply it by twelve and you have the total capacity – in this case, 3.0 litres.

The 246 Dino engine in an F2 car. The engine was given its name after Enzo's beloved son Dino who died tragically young in the 1950s. The name 'Dino' was used on all the V6 racers, and also on a beautiful V6-powered road-going GT in the late 1960s and early '70s.

Phil Hill and de Portago in a 290 MM at the 1956 Nurburgring sports car race. A lack of imagination helped when tackling the incredible 14-mile (22.5km) circuit.

Fangio at the wheel of the 860 Monza that he shared with Eugenio Castellotti in the 1956 Sebring twelve-hour race. The 860 was a 3.3-litre version of the 750 Monza. This was one of its few successes.

(Above) De Portago's 2.5-litre
625 LM abandoned beside the Le
Mans circuit as Hawthorn passes by
in a D-type. The year is 1956. A year
later Alfonso de Portago would die
in the Mille Miglia.

Peter Collins in the Lancia/Ferrari
D50 at Monza in 1956. Team-mate
Fangio's car broke down and Collins
was asked to give Fangio his, which
he did without hesitation, even though
it cost him the championship. Enzo
Ferrari never forgot this act of
sportsmanship.

(Above) The master at work: inch-perfect, Juan Manuel Fangio drifts his Lancia/ Ferrari through one of Silverstone's corners on his way to winning the 1956 British Grand Prix.

A 290 MM at the 1,000km of Nurburgring in 1956. The other 290 MM, driven by Trintignant and Musso, crashed, but this one, piloted by no fewer than four team members, came in third.

The 1956 British Grand Prix with Castellotti in the evolving Lancia/Ferrari D50 – a far better car than Ferrari's own Super Squalo 555 and 625 of 1955. Fangio won in a similar car ahead of de Portago and Collins. Castellotti finished eleventh and last.

A transaxle from a 1956 Lancia/Ferrari D50. In a transaxle the differential unit and gearbox share the same casing; by mounting the gearbox at the rear of the car the weight distribution is greatly improved.

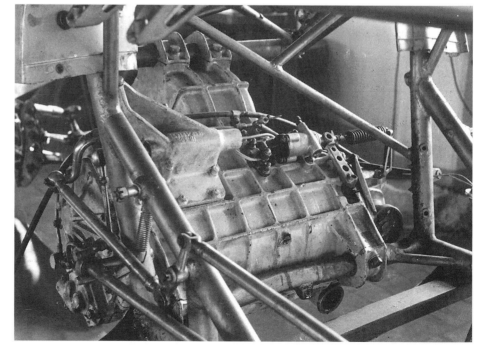

*A line-up of Lancia/
Ferrari D50s at
Siracusa in Sicily,
1956. The order runs
Fangio, Collins,
Castellotti and Musso.
Collins is in the
previous year's car,
without the fully faired
pontoons.*

*Ken Wharton in Jacques Jonneret's 3.0-litre four-cylinder 750 Monza; he
ran in fifth place before retiring. Sadly, Wharton was killed in a similar
car in January 1957 during the New Zealand Grand Prix at Ardmore.*

Paul Frere in a Lancia/Ferrari in the 1956 Belgian Grand Prix; his day job was as a motoring journalist. Several journalists have raced cars successfully, but none more so than Frere. His greatest triumph was winning Le Mans in 1960 (in a Ferrari) with Gendebien.

The start of the last race of the 1957 Tour de France, at Montlhéry. The Tour was a mixture of road-driving and circuit races. At the head of this group of varied machinery is the Marquis de Portago.

A Ferrari 860 Monza sits in a car park at Le Mans in 1956. Back then the various teams used garages dotted around the Le Mans area, and drove the cars to the circuit on the public roads.

(Below) Fangio leads the pack at Monza in 1956. Trailing him is Harry Schell in the Vanwall, then Stirling Moss in a Maserati 250 F, with Peter Collins in the number twenty-six Ferrari/Lancia D50. Parked on the grass is the Gordini with its bizarre rack of eight exhaust pipes.

A famous picture, taken by Louis Klemantaski, one of the greatest of all motor-racing photographers. Klemantaski joined Peter Collins in his Ferrari for the 1957 Mille Miglia, during which this picture was taken.

The dashing Peter Collins drives his 246 Dino to a win at the 1958 British Grand Prix at Silverstone. Less than a month later the Englishman would be dead, killed in the German Grand Prix at the unforgiving Nurburgring.

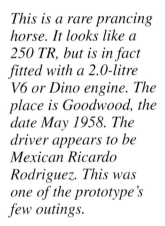

Two of the Ecurie Belge's 250 TRs at Goodwood in 1958. Soon after this the Ecurie would change its name to Ecurie Francorchamps and become one of the largest independent Ferrari teams.

This is a rare prancing horse. It looks like a 250 TR, but is in fact fitted with a 2.0-litre V6 or Dino engine. The place is Goodwood, the date May 1958. The driver appears to be Mexican Ricardo Rodriguez. This was one of the prototype's few outings.

No safety rubber-bag tanks in this 250 TR, just an aluminium tank full of high-octane fuel. The triangle of tubes is to support the hump in the boot lid, not to protect the driver's head. In any case, seatbelts were never worn.

No carbon-fibre disc brakes on this 3.0-litre Testarossa: this one has had its engine removed, as can be seen from the empty slot where the exhaust usually exits. And of course the shoe indicates that a mechanic is standing in the engine bay.

In the guts of an unidentified 1950s Ferrari single-seater. Note the de Dion tube, independent rear suspension and a transaxle; also the gated gearchange that became a Ferrari trademark and is found on all current Ferrari production cars.

Mike Hawthorn with chin on hands talks to the legendary journalist John Bolster (in the deerstalker hat) at the 1958 Moroccan Grand Prix at Casablanca. In cap and sunglasses is sometime team-mate Olivier Gendebien – like Hawthorn, in a 246 Dino.

The Sixties

Giancarlo Baghetti in a 250 Testarossa at the 1960 Sebring Twelve
Hours race, won in this year by a Porsche. Baghetti won himself a place
in the record books by winning the first grand prix that he ever entered, a
feat so far not repeated.

Stirling Moss in the
250 GT Berlinetta
entered by Rob Walker
at the 1961 Goodwood
Tourist Trophy. Moss
won the race, ahead of
Aston Martins driven
by Jim Clark and Innes
Ireland.

Phil Hill drives the 156 'shark nose' to victory in the 1961 British Grand Prix
at Aintree. Hill won the World Championship in the car, making him the first
American to win the title.

A 1961 250 GT SWB being used as its maker intended: the 250 SWB is a classic drive-it-to-the track, race-it, then drive-it-home sports car. Judging by the car park, this lucky owner is sprinting his car sometime in the mid-sixties.

(Below) A pitstop for Moss and his 250 SWB in the 1961 Goodwood TT. Looking on, above Moss's helmet, is entrant Rob Walker. His distinctive blue/white strip cars were a familiar sight at grand prix and international sports car races.

(Below) The perfect day. The beauty of the 250 SWB, the delightful atmosphere of Goodwood on a spring day, and the genius of Stirling Moss. Just to have been there ...

The start of the 1961 Tourist Trophy at Goodwood. Moss is in the Rob Walker-entered Ferrari 250 GT, with Graham Hill nearest the camera in a Porsche.

Stirling Moss crosses the line, winning the 1961 TT. A year later Moss's fantastic career would come to a premature end at the same circuit, in a Lotus at the Easter Monday meeting.

The winning 4.0-litre Testarossa of Olivier Gendebien and Phil Hill. Not only did the duo win this 1962 race, they also won together in 1958 and 1961. Gendebien won the French race a total of four times in his career.

The young Mexican Ricardo Rodriguez just before retiring his 156 F1 at Zandvoort in Holland in 1962. When Ferrari decided not to enter the non-championship grand prix in Mexico that year, Rodriguez drove a Lotus for Rob Walker instead and was killed in the race.

*Graham Hill in a 250 GTO at the 1963 Tourist Trophy at Goodwood.
Talking to Hill is entrant John Coombs, a Surrey garage owner better
known for his Jaguars than for Ferraris.*

*The 'Elde'/Pierre Dumay 250 GTO at Le Mans in 1963. Ahead is the
Lotus Elite of Wagstaff/Ferguson in the under-1.5 litre class. The number
twenty-five GTO finished fourth overall, and second in the GT class.*

(Opposite) Pierre Dumay steps out of his 250 GTO as the car is refuelled and the tyres checked for wear. The GTO was one of the greatest sports cars of all time and a perfect machine for the wealthy amateur. This car was driven back to Belgium after the race.

This could be Goodwood in the early sixties, but the modern Ferrari parked behind this 1964 250 GTO probably means that it is a Ferrari owners' club track day at the Sussex circuit some time in the late 1970s or early 1980s.

Frenchman Jean Behra in a 246 Dino at the Dutch Grand Prix of 1959, where he finished fifth. Behra was an ex-motorcycle racer and a real tiger of a driver – just the type Enzo Ferrari loved.

Kiwi Chris Amon and Scot Jackie Stewart in conversation at the 1967 British Grand Prix. Stewart is probably asking Amon for a swap as his BRM H16 was notoriously unreliable. Amon came third in the race.

A topless Jim Clark has a close look at the business end of a Ferrari 156 at the 1962 Italian Grand Prix.

(Below) *The Guichet/Parkes P2 at Le Mans in 1965. No win this year for Guichet, who won in 1964 in a 330 P shared with Sicilian ace Nino Vacarella.*

Ferrari was by no means the first racing car manufacturer to use a V12 engine, but it has almost made it its own. Only recently has Ferrari had to abandon it in F1 for a V10.

Tentative steps into aerodynamic devices on the front of this 1968-model 312 Ferrari. These small winglets would be followed by rickety flamingo-legged tall spoilers – eventually banned.

Nigel Mansell on his way to second place at the 1989 British Grand Prix. The Tifosi loved 'Il Leone' for his grit and determination in a racing car.

Mechanics wheel Chris Amon's 312 onto the grid at Jarama for the 1968 Spanish Grand Prix. Amon started on pole, and led the mid-section of the race before retiring from a race that had only five finishers at the flag.

The Willy Mairesse and 'Beurlys' P4 has undergone some body adjustments at Le Mans in 1967. Mairesse was not unknown to knock a few corners off a car en route. The words 'fear' and 'give up' were not in his vocabulary.

A Ferrari 158 nosecone sits on the tarmac at Monaco in 1965. Neither team drivers John Surtees nor Lorenzo Bandini has number 20 in the race, so this is obviously a pre-race spare.

Amon at speed at Monza. Monza was a hugely fast circuit in those days, where the art of slipstreaming was everything. John Surtees won the race in a Honda at an average speed of 140.5mph (233kph).

(Below) *Ferrari mechanics work on Jacky Ickx' and Chris Amon's 312s at the 1968 Belgian Grand Prix, in the days when the public were not kept away from the fun.*

Perhaps Maranello's best loved son – Canadian Gilles Villeneuve. Even now, over ten years after his death, he is still worshipped in Italy. He didn't win the championship for Ferrari, but everyone loved the style in which he was trying to do so.

A Ferrari 330 P4 shows off its 4.0-litre V12 engine at the 1967 BOAC 1,000km at Brands Hatch. Number six was driven by Jackie Stewart and Chris Amon.

Chris Amon's 312 visits the pits at Monza in the 1967 Grand Prix. He finished seventh, after pitting to have a handling problem sorted out.

John Surtees' Ferrari 156 receives attention in the pits at the 1963 Belgian Grand Prix at Spa. The verdict was a broken fuel injection pipe and his race was over.

The racing numbers are carefully applied to the nose of a 330 P2 at Le Mans in 1965.

(Below) *No digital readout, no banks of steering wheel-mounted switches, just a wood-rimmed wheel and a trio of gauges in this V8 1.5-litre Ferrari Tipo 158 F1 car.*

Willy Mairesse and 'Beurlys' in a road-going 275 GTB at Le Mans in 1965. The car was entered by Ecurie Francorchamps, one of the major privateer Ferrari teams in the 1960s. The pair finished third.

Rene Arnoux drove for Ferrari from 1983 to '84, though fans will remember him best for his dice (in a Renault) with Gilles Villeneuve at Dijon in 1979.

Mike Parkes in the 330 P2 which he shared with Jean Guichet at Le Mans in 1965, the year that Jochen Rindt and Masten Gregory won in a Ferrari 250 LM.

(Below) The Courage/Pike 275 GTB at Le Mans in 1965. The car was entered by the British Ferrari importers Maranello Concessionaires, whose trademark blue nose can be seen on the car.

Peter Collins sweeps through one of Silverstone's open corners on his way to a win in the 1958 British Grand Prix in his Dino 246 Ferrari.

John Surtees leads Swede Jo Bonnier's Cooper T60 at Monaco in 1963. Surtees' Ferrari 156 finished fourth, while Bonnier came in seventh, six laps behind.

A Ferrari 156 receives a refill at Monaco in 1963. Look where that fuel is going – into a tank right above the driver's knees. In the days before puncture-proof rubber bag tanks, too.

(Below) Another Ferrari 275 GTB at Le Mans. This time in 1967, driven by Steinemann and Spoerry. Rico Steinemann was better known as a Porsche driver, and later became Porsche team manager.

The Scarfiotti/Parkes 330 P4 at Le Mans in 1967. Ferrari fielded a huge array of cars at Le Mans that year, but Ford still won. This pair came in second, four laps behind the winners.

The Parkes/Maglioli Ferrari 250 P passes one of the infamous Le Mans sand traps during the 1963 race. The pairing finished third, with victory going to another 250 P driven by Scarfiotti and Bandini.

John Surtees motions to the mechanics from the cockpit of his 1964 158 at the Dutch Grand Prix. He came second in the race, a lap behind. Surtees finished the year as World Champion.

Phil Hill in the last of the front-engined Ferrari grand prix cars, the Dino 246, at Monaco in 1959. Hill finished fourth, despite spinning three times.

The Courage/Pike 275 GTB at speed at Le Mans in 1966. The 275 GTB was the last of the dual-purpose Ferraris – at home on road and track. It was also one of the most beautiful Ferrari GT cars.

If anyone can break Ferrari's world championship drought then it is Michael Schumacher. If Ferrari can't win with a driver of his genius on board, then there is a real problem.

Lorenzo Bandini is surely a perfect name for a works' Ferrari driver; he looked the part, too. Here Bandini is on his way to winning the 1964 Austrian Grand Prix in a Tipo 156, his first grand prix victory.

American amateur Sterling Hamil slings his 250 GT into a corner, hotly pursued by a somewhat damaged Chevrolet Corvette, with a diminutive Abarth following in third.

(Opposite) The winning car at Le Mans in 1964, a 275 P driven by Jean Guichet and Nino Vacarella. Vacarella was a Sicilian schoolmaster whose speciality was naturally the Targa Florio. However, this victory at Le Mans is one of his several international victories.

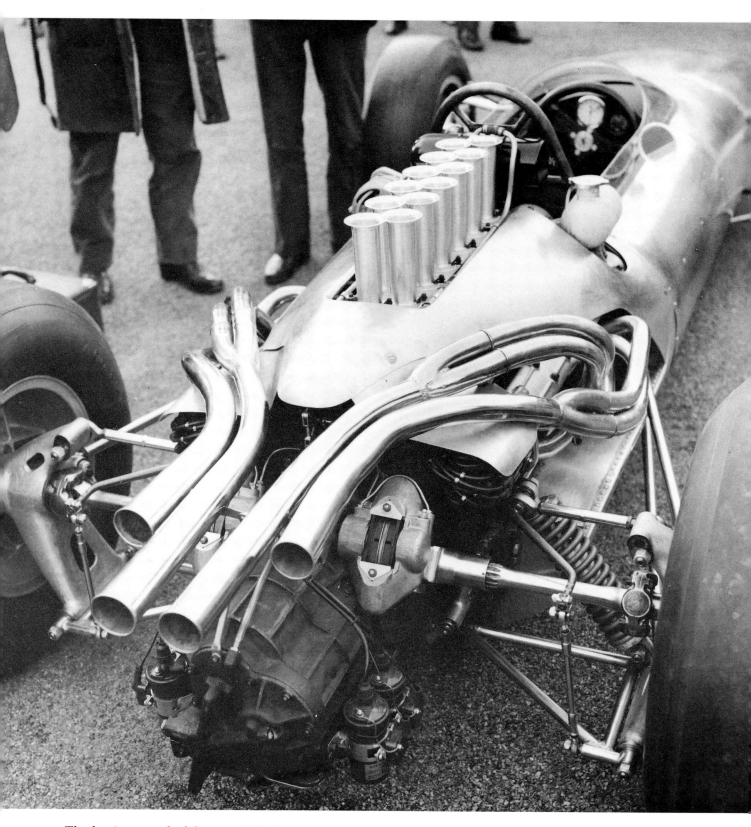

The business end of the new 312 F1 car. If championship points were awarded for looks and sound, then this Ferrari would have scored the maximum. The next year it had to deal with the Cosworth DFV engine, as Ferrari engines would have to for the next dozen or so years.

The 250 LM (actually a 3.3-litre model, so technically it should be a 275 LM) was often used on the road. It wasn't the most practical of road cars, but a trip to compete in a hill climb would have been a joy.

This rarity is the 250 LM, shown at the 1965 Geneva Motor Show, one of two LMs built by the factory as road cars. This one had electric windows and the additional roof-mounted gull-wing doors to aid entry. Note also the huge plastic rear window.

A 330 P2/P3 sneaks its nose out of a workshop. The 4.4-litre, 380bhp P2/P3 was built by the factory for the major independent teams. It was simple, fast and relatively easy to maintain – and gorgeous.

Jochen Rindt was not a big fan of long-distance racing, but that did not stop him from driving the life out of this 250 LM to give him and Masten Gregory victory at Le Mans in 1965.

John Surtees at speed at Silverstone in the 312 F1. This was the first year of the 3.0-litre formula and Surtees' last year at Ferrari; he left the team after a bitter dispute early in the season. Surtees is the only man to have won World Championships on both two and four wheels, a record that is likely never to be broken.

The John Love/Paul Hawkins P4 spider in the pits at Kyalami during the Rand Nine Hours race. The car suffered repeatedly from a wet ignition system and made several long pitstops to be dried out.

The factory P4 of Mike Parkes and Ludovico Scarfiotti finished second, behind Foyt and Gurney in a Ford GT40 MK 4 and ahead of 'Beurlys' and Mairesse in the Ecurie Francorchamps P4 at Le Mans in 1967.

A Ferrari 250 MM at rest outside the Egeskov veteran vehicle museum in Denmark. Earlier Ferraris were hand-built machines and often varied one from another. This car has at some time received a new front end.

In 1965 Pininfarina produced this very much road-going 250 LM Berlinetta. Note the bumperettes and the gill-like covers over the rear air intakes.

A 330 P3 at speed in the rain at Monza in 1966: it won this race with Surtees and Parkes driving. This was a high point in a year that saw Ferrari trounced at Le Mans by a Ford GT40 one-two-three.

Ferrari unveils its new F1 car for the 1966 season. It was the first year of the 3.0-litre formula and the 312 promised a great deal. Unfortunately, it failed to deliver, so perhaps they should have left the slicks on.

Ludovico Scarfiotti was most at home in sports cars and on hill climbs, although he did also make several grand prix outings for Ferrari. This is his most successful: a win in the 1966 Italian Grand Prix in a 312.

The business end of Bandini's 312 at Monaco in 1967. Bandini was holding second place when, towards the end of the race, he crashed at the seafront chicane. The car was consumed in a terrible fire and Bandini succumbed to his injuries and died several days later.

*Chris Amon corners his thirty-six-valve V12-powered 312 through a
corner of the Le Mans-Bugatti circuit in the 1967 French Grand Prix.
Amon is considered to be one of the most talented, but also one of the
most unlucky drivers ever because he never won a grand prix but came
so close, so often.*

*(Opposite) Jackie Stewart in a rare Ferrari outing, in the 1967 BOAC
1,000km Castellotti at Brands Hatch. He shared the 330 P4 with Chris
Amon and they finished second behind the Phil Hill/Mike Spence Chaparral.*

The somewhat battered P4 of the Belgian driver Willy Mairesse and 'Beurlys' at Le Mans in 1967; the pair came in third, behind two GT40s. Mairesse had no concept of fear whatsoever, although by this time a succession of serious crashes had dulled his talent.

Ferrari's 1967 330 P4 spider is unquestionably one of the most beautiful sports racing cars of all time.

The Mike Parkes/ Ludovico Scarfiotti Ferrari P4 at Le Mans in 1967. The race was won by A.J. Foyt and Dan Gurney in a Ford MK 4, although Parkes and Scarfiotti were gaining on the Ford in the last two hours on Sunday – it was not enough, however.

Ferrari (left) talks to an official at a race in the late 1960s. Ferrari rarely attended races personally, and in his later life would only be seen at his home grand prix in Italy.

(Below) Ferrari engineering genius Mauro Forghieri wheels out the 166 F2 car in 1968. The 1.6-litre V6-powered car was driven by Amon, Ickx, Derek Bell and many others, though it was, somewhat surprisingly, Tino Brambilla who took it to its first victory at Hockenheim in October.

Ernesto 'Tino' Brambilla taking his 166 F2 car to a sixth place in the Wills Trophy at Thruxton in 1968. Note the unusual aerodynamic wheel discs.

Hill climbing was serious stuff in the sixties. This is the designer-built car that Peter Schetty used to win the 1969 European Hill Climb Championship. Schetty went on to manage Ferrari's sports car team.

The four works' 512 Ss line up for the start of the 1970 Le Mans. The race was a disaster for Ferrari: of their eleven cars entered, only three managed to finish, and one of those was unclassified.

Two 512 Ss at Le Mans in 1970, a short while before things went horribly wrong for Ferrari: Reine Wisell slowed his 512 S because of oil on the windscreen, and Regazzoni drove into him in his 512. Then Parkes hit him, and finally along came Derek Bell in his 512, hit the debris and turned his car over.

This 1971 312 B is now in the Donington Collection, a haven for lovers of grand prix machines. Here it is shown outside – if the numbering is correct, it is ex-Jacky Ickx.

*The fifth-placed NART-entered 365 GTB/4 Daytona driven by Lloyd Grossman and
Luigi Chinetti jnr (son of the NART founder) leads the Enever/Edwards Lola T212
and two Porsche 911s at Le Mans in 1971.*

*Ex-racer, team owner and now big businessman, Roger Penske (far left) watches as
English driver David Hobbs chats to Mark Donohue in a 512 M. The 512 M was a further
development of the 512 S. Donohue later died at the wheel of a Penske F1 car.*

(Opposite) The young and gifted Jacky Ickx in his flat-twelve 312 B2 in the Spanish Grand Prix in 1971. Ickx raced for Ferrari for four seasons but the cars were never quite up to his talent. He found success later in his career with the Rothmans Porsches.

The bizarre shovel-nose front on this 1972 312 B3 was tested late in the season, but it was never raced. It would have made the commentator's life easier, if nothing else.

Le Mans regular and ex-BRM F1 driver Francois Migault driving a 365 GTB/4 Daytona to fifth place in the 1972 Le Mans. The car was entered by Charles Pozzi, the French Ferrari importer.

*The Swede Ronnie Peterson takes the flag in Buenos Aires in a 312 PB;
he shared the car with Australian Tim Schenken. Ferrari won the
Championship of Makes that year, a high point in a lean decade.*

*A spin for the 365
GTB/4 Daytona of
Andruet/Bichet in the
1972 Tour de France.
The Daytona was never
the ideal competition
car as it is big and
heavy to drive, but it is
nonetheless extremely
powerful.*

84

It takes something special to drive a powerful sports car around a wet Nurburgring, and Ronnie Peterson was very special, his car control being of the highest calibre. He won this race, but no one knows whether he enjoyed himself.

Arturo Merzario's works' 312 PB gets a push from the mechanics for a practice session for the 1972 Targa Floria. Merzario, with co-driver Sandro Munari, won the event. This sort of practice was always risky as the roads were still open.

That bulge on the side of the Merzario/ Munari 312 PB covers an extra fuel tank to take the car further on the 40-mile (65km) Sicilian road course. The Targa Florio is no more, but the memory of this incredible road race lives on in the minds of all who were fortunate to take part in it or to witness it.

The class-winning Daytona at Le Mans in 1972 stops in the pits for fuel.
The drivers of this Charles Pozzi-entered 365 GTB/4 were Andruet and
Ballot-Lena. Francois Migault in another Daytona finished fifth.

The trouble with big road-going sports cars like the Daytona is that they often suffer from the opposite to downforce. This can be alarming when travelling flat-out on, say, the Mulsanne Straight at Le Mans. This simple spoiler was designed to keep the car's rear end better planted.

The Ickx/Andretti stops for tyres and fuel in the 1972 Sebring Twelve Hour race. Sebring was an airfield circuit that just a few times a year was turned into an international race circuit, rough and bouncy and a real car-breaker. This particular model survived, however, and finished first.

Andretti rounds Brands' Bottom Bend in the 312 P which he shared with Jacky Ickx, to win the BOAC 1,000km at the Kent circuit. Ronnie Petersen and Tim Schenken were second in an identical car.

*Ferrari had a great season in 1972, giving
major rival Alfa Romeo a severe beating in
the Championship of Makes that year. Here
Ickx (right) and Andretti (second from left)
collect the silverware at Brands Hatch.*

*Australian Tim Schenken leads the 312 P of
Brian Redman and Clay Regazzoni at the
BOAC 1,000km. These were the days when
grand prix stars took part in all forms of
racing, and were still approachable.*

'Quick' Vic Elford hustling a Daytona in the Tour de France in 1972.
Elford was an ex-rally driver who excelled in sports cars. In 1972 he had
a grim season with Alfa Romeo in the Tipo 33 sports car, losing on a
regular basis to the Scuderia's 312 Ps.

The Redman/Regazzoni 312 P during the BOAC 1,000km at Brands
Hatch in 1972. It looks as though Regazzoni might be suffering from a
bit of understeer, from the manner in which his front tyre is loaded up.

Another good result for the Scuderia's sports-car wing in 1972 as Tim Schenken, sharing with Swede Ronnie Petersen, brings in the 312 P in third place in the Monza 1,000km.

A very well-used 365 GTB4 Daytona at Le Mans in 1972. Driven by Americans Sam Posey and Tony Adamowicx, the Daytona finished sixth. By this time Ferrari's official participation at Le Mans was nearly over, leaving private teams to uphold the honour of the prancing horse.

Clay Regazzoni in his 312 P sweeps past Rob Grant's Datsun 240 Z in the Kyalami Nine Hours in 1972. Kyalami used to be a dramatic circuit much liked by drivers (the climate helped), but today it is a shadow of its former self, emasculated in the name of safety.

Sandro Munari flings his 312 P through a Sicilian village en route to winning the 1972 Targa Florio. Munari was better known as a rally driver, and this was in fact the ideal background to have for the dusty and challenging Targa. Today he works in communications at Lamborghini.

Jacky Ickx leading the early stages of the 1972 British Grand Prix in the boxer-engined 312 B3. His pole position and lead came to nothing, however, when the twelve-cylinder Ferrari motor lost oil pressure. Ickx won the next grand prix, the German, but this was his only win of the season.

(Opposite) Brian Redman has this bit of the Nurburgring to himself in the 1972 1,000km. Lancastrian Redman is one of the most charming people in racing, and very capable. Mario Andretti rates him as one of the top ten drivers he has ever known.

Regazzoni leads Ickx's similar 312 P during the 1972 BOAC 1,000km at Brands Hatch. This was the last year of that excellent event, although it did make a brief reappearance as the British Airways' 1000km in 1974.

Brian Redman on his way to second place in the Buenos Aires 1,000km in 1972, in a 312 P that he shared with Clay Regazzoni. Note how much air there is between the Ferrari's belly and the tarmac; ground effects were still a long way off.

Jacky Ickx at speed in a 312 B3 at Silverstone in the 1973 British Grand Prix. He finished eighth. His F1 had started to falter by then, but he went on to be one of the highest winning sports car drivers of all time.

Jody Scheckter in his 312 T4. Sheckter's early reputation as a 'wild kid' – he wiped out half the field in the 1973 British Grand Prix – had passed by 1979. He won the Driver's Championship for Ferrari – the company's last, in fact.

Jacky Ickx and his flat-twelve 312 B3 pass the harbour at Monaco in the 1973 Grand Prix. Ferrari was suffering a non-winning period and Ickx's patience ran out a few races later. He freelanced for a few teams before joining Lotus in 1974.

Ickx flies through Tertre Rouge during the 1973 Le Mans in his 312 P. The 312 P used what was essentially the 3.0-litre Formula One car's engine. Ickx shared the car with Yorkshireman Brian Redman, one of racing's most underrated talents.

New pieces were often tested during the course of a season. Here the Merzario/Carlos Pace 312 P has a new airbox and rear bodywork for the Nurburgring 1,000km in 1973. Behind it is the winning 312 P of Ickx and Redman.

The old and magnificent Oesterreichring. Ickx was outclassed in the 1973 1,000km at the circuit by the Matra MS670s of Pescarolo/Larrouse and of Beltoise/Cervert who finished first and second respectively.

The Vic Elford/Ballot-Lena 365 GTB/4, hotly pursued by a Porsche 911 Carrera, and following behind that, Mike Hailwood in the Gulf Mirage sports prototype. The Ferrari finished sixth overall.

The Ferrari 312 P of Arturo Merzario and Carlos Pace kicks up a storm at Le Mans in 1973. The car finished second behind the winning Matra of Pescarolo and Larousse. Pace was later tragically killed in a light plane crash in Brazil.

The long tail-section on this Ferrari 312 PB gives a clue as to the event which the car is attending: Le Mans. Actually this picture was taken during the test weekend that took place several months before the June race itself.

And (below) one-two is how Ickx (in number 1) and Merzario finished the 1973 1,000km of the Nurburgring. Results such as this weren't happening for Ferrari in Formula One, however – still, Lauda was on his way.

Jacky Ickx starts the 1973 grand prix season with a fourth place in Argentina. It was his last season with the Scuderia – indeed his patience with the team ran out towards the end of the season. His future success lay in sports cars with Porsche.

(Right) A 330P shows off its regulation spare wheel. Those square sections in the rear lowermost of the raised tail section are actually the luggage compartments – again fitted to comply with regulations.

The parked aircraft give a clue as to this circuit's name: it is Sebring in Florida, for most of the year an airport. The circuit was laid out using the runways and taxiways. Here Ickx leads a quick Porsche and a not-so-quick Porsche 914 road car.

Clay Regazzoni at Monaco in 1975. Rega was in his second year back at Ferrari after a year off in the Marlboro BRM team in 1973. He won the Italian Grand Prix in 1975, but his greatest value to the team was as a foil to Niki Lauda.

A rare dry practice session for the non-championship 1974 Race of Champions at Brands Hatch: Clay Regazzoni runs wide onto the green, while Lauda keeps his 312 B3 on the road.

Niki Lauda endures the rain at the 1974 Race of Champions at Brands Hatch. It was the era of the tall airboxes – later outlawed – and enormous rear tyres. The car is a 312 B3.

Gianclaudio 'Clay' Regazzoni at work in his 312 B3 in miserable conditions at the 1974 Race of Champions at Brands Hatch. Ickx won in a Lotus 72. Regga was a long-time Ferrari works' driver. His career ended at Long Beach in 1980 with an accident that has put him into a wheelchair for the rest of his life.

Close on Niki Lauda at the 1974 Race of Champions. Lauda took Ferrari out of the doldrums a year later. A year after that he was at death's door after his horrific accident on the Nurburgring: the German circuit was never used again for grand prix racing.

(Right) Ickx at the 1973 Spanish Grand Prix at Montjuich Park. He pitted with brake trouble and as a result finished last, six laps behind.

Niki Lauda proved to be a saviour to the Italian team, in 1975 bringing to an end their bleak period of no wins with the first championship success since Surtees in 1964. This is Lauda the year before in Argentina, when he finished second.

A wet, miserable Race of Champions at Brands Hatch in 1974. Clay Regazzoni gets the better start in his 312 B3 Ferrari, ahead of James Hunt in his Hesketh 308. Jacky Ickx won the race in a Lotus 72.

Lauda in the 312 T in 1975, his championship year. The 'T' stood for transversale because the gearbox was transversal instead of in line; it allowed designer Mauro Forghieri to make the 312 T more compact than before, and in 1975 it was a winner.

The Eighties

One of the few drivers to touch Enzo's heart was Gilles Villeneuve. The Canadian knew only one way to drive, and that was flat out. Here he is in a 312 T5 at Brands Hatch in the 1980 British Grand Prix. His death when qualifying for the 1982 Dutch Grand Prix devastated Ferrari – and Italy.

Villeneuve at Silverstone in 1981; he spun off. To many he was what Formula One is all about – and one thing you knew was that he would always put on a great show. He may be gone, but in F1 and Ferrari circles, he will never be forgotten.

*Italian Michele Alboreto in his 1.5-litre turbocharged Ferrari F1/87/88
at the British Grand Prix in 1988. It was his last season with the
Scuderia, having joined in 1984. His first year was his best, despite being
let down by engine problems more than once.*

*Alboreto at the 1988
British Grand Prix on
wet tyres during a
downpour. The finesse
required to handle
these all-or-nothing
turbocharged cars in
such conditions was
considerable.*

111

Alboreto's team-mate Austrian Gerhard Berger started the 1988 British Grand Prix in pole position, but poor fuel consumption – he had to turn the boost down to make it last – meant that he finished ninth, a lap behind.

Nigel Mansell's beginning with the Ferrari team in 1989 could not have got off to a better start: he won first time out (in Brazil) and here, in the British Grand Prix in the same year, he finished second in his 3.5-litre V12 640. Unreliability ruined an otherwise successful season.

(Opposite) Henry Ford was perhaps the most important man in the history of the car, in that he brought the motor car to the ordinary person. Enzo Ferrari, however, brought passion to many and extraordinary cars to the fortunate few. Modern Formula One would be a shadow of itself had he never been born.

The People

Even more than Stirling Moss, Mike Hawthorn epitomized the British racing driver. Hawthorn would always wear a bow-tie when racing. He joined the Scuderia in 1953, driving a Ferrari 500. Here Hawthorn (left) talks to Earl Howe at Goodwood in 1953.

Hawthorn, complete with spotted dickie-bow, his trademark, talks with Stirling Moss just before the International Trophy race at Goodwood in 1956. Although Moss was the more talented driver, it was Hawthorn who became the World Champion.

(Opposite) In 1958, Hawthorn became the first ever British World Champion. He retired at the end of the year, to get married and concentrate on his garage business. Tragically he was killed in a road accident in January 1959.

Peter Collins, right, with Luigi Musso at Monaco in 1956. More than a little handsome, Collins and his friend Mike Hawthorn used to live life to the full, and Hawthorn was devastated when his close friend was killed at the Nurburgring in 1958.

Peter Collins joined the Ferrari team in 1956 – the year of the Lancia/ Ferraris – as Fangio's team-mate. Collins was a true sportsman. At the 1956 Italian Grand Prix he handed his car over to Fangio (his had broken down) thereby giving up the chance of winning the champion-ship himself.

Nuvolari (third from the right) meets the US ambassador (right) at a motor show in 1950. Three years later 'The Mantovan Lion' would be dead; he was a chain-smoker and had been in poor health for many years.

The legendary Tazio Nuvolari stands beside his Scuderia Ferrari Alfa Romeo and directs refuelling. Enzo Ferrari had enormous respect for Nuvolari, and rated him as one of the all-time greats. He joined the Scuderia in 1929.

Alberto Ascari (with
the goggles round his
neck) was the son of a
famous racing father:
Antonio Ascari, killed
when young Alberto
was seven years old.
Alberto himself died
young, at the wheel of a
Ferrari sports car he
was testing at Monza in
May 1955.

The sticking plaster on
Alberto Ascari's chin is
probably covering a
graze which he received
when he famously
launched his Lancia/
Ferrari D50 – similar
to the one pictured here
– into the harbour at
Monte Carlo in the
1955 Grand Prix
de Monaco, an
achievement for which
he earned great renown.

118

Phil Hill's chief claim to fame is that he was the first American to win the F1 World Championship. Hill's career started in the US, club racing an MG. He first raced sports cars for the Scuderia, but in 1958 was given the chance to drive the grand prix cars.

Hill won the championship in 1961, despite the fact that he won only two races that year, in Belgium and Italy, the latter being the race which decided the championship. It was not an occasion for celebration, however, as team-mate Wolfgang Von Tripps lost his life that day.

119

Whatever Hill is saying, it is unlikely to be complimentary. The man in the cap is Carlo Chiti, ex-Ferrari engineer and owner of the woefully unsuccessful ATS team that Hill drove for in 1963. His grand prix career was effectively over.

Chris Amon drove for the Scuderia through 1967 to the end of 1969. He also drove sports cars for Ferrari, including the fearsome but outclassed 612 and 712s in the CanAm Championship in the United States and Canada.

Mario Andretti once said that if Chris Amon entered the funeral business 'people would quit dying'. Amon had a huge talent, but he never seemed to achieve the wins he deserved. The New Zealander is without doubt the most talented driver never to have won a grand prix.

A serious-looking John Surtees with hands on hips. Surtees is the only man ever to have won World Championships on two and four wheels, and his arrival at Ferrari in 1963 reversed the team's fortunes. The following year Surtees took the title in the 1.5-litre 158.

Jacky Ickx was another driver who certainly deserved to win the World Championship. A genius in the wet, he first drove for Ferrari in 1968 when he was still only twenty-three. After a season away from the Italian team in 1969, Ickx then rejoined it and drove for Maranello until he joined Lotus in 1974.

Jacky Ickx takes the laurels at the German Grand Prix at the Nurburgring in 1972. In second place (to Ickx's right) is team-mate Clay Regazzoni, and in the right of the picture the Swede Ronnie Peterson who drove a March to third.

A Ferrari one-two at the 1973 Nurburgring 1,000km. Jacky Ickx (centre) and Brian Redman (right) were first, Carlos Pace (left) and a missing Arturo Merzario were second. Both pairs were in Ferrari 312 Ps.

Australian Tim Schenken gives the photographer a signal as he and Ronnie Peterson share victory at the Nurburgring 1,000km in 1972. Schenken's F1 career was a disappointment, but several victories in the Ferrari sports car team (usually paired with Peterson) partly made up for that.

Mario Andretti (left of the bunnygirl) and Jacky Ickx (with the trophy) win the 1972 Sebring Twelve Hours for Ferrari. Ickx, from the look on his face, is perhaps trying to remember the bunnygirl's telephone number.

Austrian Niki Lauda will always be remembered in Maranello, because he took the team out of its victory drought, winning the World Championship for Ferrari in 1975 and again in 1977, the latter a year after his nearly fatal accident in the 1976 German Grand Prix.

Swiss driver Gianclaudio 'Clay' Regazzoni had a reputation as somewhat wild in his early career. He had a long career at Ferrari, driving six seasons for the team. His career finished at Long Beach in 1980 when he was paralysed in a horrific accident in an Ensign.

Ex-racer and Ferrari sports car team manager Peter Schetty with the 1972 Targa Florio-winning 312 PB, driven by Arturo Merzario and Sandro Munari. A great car, and a great race.

Frenchman Didier Pironi raced two seasons for Ferrari, both of them alongside the great and beloved Gilles Villeneuve. Pironi's career in cars came to an end at Hockenheim when a serious practice accident smashed his ankles. He subsequently took up powerboat racing, and was killed in one in 1987.

Four-time World Champion Alain Prost is one of the most talented drivers to race for the Ferrari team. Nicknamed the 'Professor', Prost was very undramatic to watch because he made it look so easy. He was, however, extremely quick.